SOOKIEANDIVY

Sookie and Ivy

EVERY DAY IS A CELEBRATION!

JANI OJA

Don't miss our other book, *Friends Forever!*

© 2024 by Jani Oja and Fox Chapel Publishing Company, Inc.

Sookie and Ivy Every Day Is a Celebration! is an original work, first published in 2024 by Fox Chapel Publishing Company, Inc.

All rights reserved. No part of this publication may be reproduced, stored in a retrieval system or transmitted, in any form or by any means, electronic, mechanical, photocopying, recording or otherwise, without the prior written permission of the copyright holders.

ISBN 978-1-4971-0527-0

The Cataloging-in-Publication Data is on file with the Library of Congress.

To learn more about the other great books from Fox Chapel Publishing, or to find a retailer near you, call toll-free

800-457-9112

or send mail to

903 Square Street

Mount Joy, PA 17552

or visit us at www.FoxChapelPublishing.com.

We are always looking for talented authors. To submit an idea, please send a brief inquiry to

acquisitions@foxchapelpublishing.com.

Printed in China

First printing

Sookie

Ivy

Hi There

Allow us to introduce ourselves. We're Sookie and Ivy, senior hat models and pawfessional food critics with a knack for making people smile. We were rescued as small girls, and now we spend our days in luxury, wearing silly hats that are designed and handmade by our mom. We're the ultimate besties, and we've shared every adventure for over a decade. Try not to be jealous, and don't let our serious faces fool you—we love the attention and are ready to "sit, stay, and cro-slay" as soon as our mom grabs her camera (and the treatos!). This book is a celebration of our timeless friendship, and the beauty of friendship all around the world!

"Wherever you go, no matter what the weather, always bring your own sunshine."

–Anthony J. D'Angelo

SOOKIEANDIVY

"Dogs are not our whole life,
but they make our lives whole."

–ROGER CARAS

"The way I see it, if you want the rainbow, you gotta put up with the rain."

–DOLLY PARTON

"In a world where you can be anything, be kind."

–CLARE POOLEY

"You and me, we're soymates."

–SOOKIE AND IVY

"Try to be a rainbow in someone's cloud."

–MAYA ANGELOU

"You can't make everyone happy.
You're not pizza."

–UNKNOWN

"You've got to be kiwiing me."

–Sookie and Ivy

"There are always flowers
for those who want to see them."

–HENRI MATISSE

"Life is like a bowl of spaghetti.
Every once in a while, you get a meatball."

–SHARON CREECH

"Live every week like it's Shark Week."

–TRACY JORDAN, *30 ROCK*

"What would life be if we had no courage
to attempt anything?"

–Vincent van Gogh

"It is the sweet, simple things of life which are the real ones after all."

–Laura Ingalls Wilder

"There's power in looking silly
and not caring that you do."

–AMY POEHLER

BING BONG

"Be yourself. Unless you can be a unicorn.
In that case, you should always be a unicorn."

–ELLE LOTHLORIEN

"To plant a garden is to dream of tomorrow."

–AUDREY HEPBURN

"It simply isn't an adventure worth telling
if there aren't any dragons."

–SARAH BAN BREATHNACH

SOOKIEANDIVY

"What's right is what's left
if you do everything else wrong."

–Robin Williams

"Santa, don't forget the Grinch.
I know he's mean and hairy and smelly.
His hands might be cold and clammy,
but I think he's actually kinda . . . sweet."

–CINDY LOU WHO, *HOW THE GRINCH STOLE CHRISTMAS*

"You can't buy happiness,
but you can rescue it."

–SOOKIE AND IVY

"Don't get your tinsel in a tangle!"

–UNKNOWN

"We don't make mistakes,
just happy little accidents."

–Bᴏʙ Rᴏss

"When life gives you lemons, friggin bye."

–SOOKIE AND IVY

"Happiness is a warm puppy."

–Charles M. Schulz

"Normal is not something to aspire to,
it's something to get away from."

–JODIE FOSTER

SOOKIEANDIVY

"Some day you will be old enough
to start reading fairy tales again."

–C.S. LEWIS

"You're one in a melon."

–Sookie and Ivy

SOOKIEANDIVY

"Joy is the simplest form of gratitude."

–KARL BARTH

"The world would be a nicer place
if everyone had the ability to love
as unconditionally as a dog."

–M.K. CLINTON

"Beware; for I am fearless
and therefore powerful."

–MARY SHELLEY

About the Author and Doggos

Jani Oja was born in Finland and currently resides in Massachusetts with her husband and two rescue dogs, Sookie and Ivy. She is a self-taught crochet artist and hobby photographer, and shares Sookie and Ivy's adventures on social media to their two million supporters. Sookie and Ivy were both adopted from animal shelters in Florida, and Ivy, in particular, came from a rough beginning. The pair are lovingly known as "the gorls," and Jani hopes their silly videos and photo content can help teach people to not judge dogs based on their appearance. The gorls were destined to spread smiles, and are tail-wagging ready to create content as soon as Jani starts to set up their recording area. To see Sookie and Ivy's full hat collection spanning over 100 sets, connect with Jani on social media (@sookieandivy on all platforms).